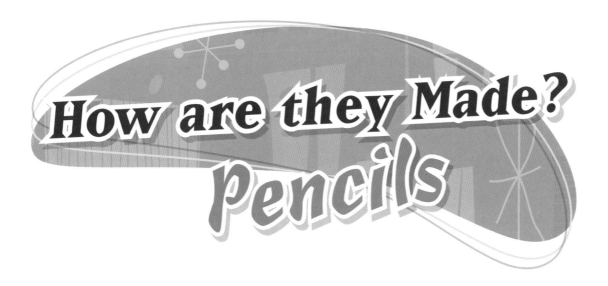

How are they Made?
Pencils

Wendy Blaxland

MACMILLAN
LIBRARY

First published in 2008 by
MACMILLAN EDUCATION AUSTRALIA PTY LTD
15–19 Claremont Street, South Yarra 3141

Visit our website at www.macmillan.com.au or go directly to www.macmillanlibrary.com.au

Associated companies and representatives throughout the world.

National Library of Australia
Cataloguing-in-Publication data

Blaxland, Wendy, 1949-
    Pencils / author, Wendy Blaxland.
    South Yarra, Vic. : Macmillan Education, 2008.
    ISBN: 978 1 4202 6412 8 (hbk.)
    Blaxland, Wendy, 1949- How are they made?
    Includes index.
    Pencils--Juvenile literature.
    Pencil industry--Juvenile literature.
674.88

Edited by Anna Fern
Cover design, text design and page layout by Cristina Neri, Canary Graphic Design
Photo research by Legend Images
Map by Damien Demaj, DEMAP; modified by Cristina Neri, Canary Graphic Design

Printed in China

Acknowledgements
The author would like to thank the following people for their expert advice: Chris Brown, Faber-Castell Australia; Alan
Cole, Chairman, Museum of Writing, University of London; and Mandy Knowlson, Staedtler Australia.

The author and the publisher are grateful to the following for permission to reproduce copyright material:

Front cover photograph: Loose coloured pencils © Anton Zhukov/iStockphoto; coloured pencils in wire holder
© Rafał Głębowski/iStockphoto. Images repeated throughout title.

Photos courtesy of:
© Ellen Isaacs/Alamy, **24**; The Cumberland Pencil Company, **4** (left), **5** (top left, top right), **8**, **22** (bottom), **23**, **26**; Digital
Vision, **30** (bottom); Faber-Castell, **7** (both), **9**, **10** (bottom), **16** (right), **17**, **18**, **19**, **20**, **21** (top), **25**; Photodisc/Getty
mages, **28**; Dael Honermann, **14**; © Jill Fromer/iStockphoto, **3** (bottom), **10** (top), **13** (bottom), **15** (top), **16** (left), **21**
(bottom), **22** (top), **29** (bottom), **30** (top); Doug Martin, www.pencilpages.com, **4** (right); MEA Photo, **11**; Photodisc/S
Meltzer/PhotoLink, **5** (bottom); Photodisc/Tracy Montana/PhotoLink, **29** (top); Photolibrary/Andre Baranowski, **27**.

Headshot illustrations accompanying textboxes throughout title © Russell Tate/iStockphoto.

Contents

Glossary words

When a word is printed in **bold**, you can look up its meaning in the Glossary on page 31.

From raw materials to products

Everything we use is made from raw materials from the Earth. These are called natural resources. People take natural resources and make them into useful products.

Pencils

Pencils are used for writing and for drawing. A writing pencil is usually made up of a thin black stick encased in a wooden tube. In drawing pencils the stick is coloured.

The main raw materials used to make writing pencils are **graphite** and wood. Graphite is a black mineral dug from the earth, which is mixed with clay and baked to make the pencil core. Wood is cut from trees and shaped by machines to make a casing or shaft around the graphite core.

As well as graphite and wood, colouring **pigments** are used to make coloured pencils and to paint the casings.

Six-sided pencil casings allow the user to grip them more firmly and have greater control when drawing.

Graphite is a dark, slippery material.

LAKELAND Colourthin
12 fine, precise coloured pencils
12
Quality colouring pencils for the aspiring artist
from the makers of
DERWENT

Oblong carpenters' pencils can be sharpened to a chisel-shaped edge that makes it easier to write on wood than with a fine-pointed pencil.

Different pencils are made for different purposes.

Why do we need pencils?

Pencils are one of the most useful tools in history because they help so many people to learn to read and write, create art and sketch down ideas.

Pencils have some advantages over pens. Marks made with pencils can be varied more easily than those made by ink or ballpoint pens. Pencil marks are also more easily rubbed out than ink marks. Pencils can write upside down, but most ink pens cannot.

An average pencil can be sharpened 17 times.

Question & Answer

Where does the word 'pencil' come from?

The word 'pencil' comes from *peniculus*, which is Latin for 'little tail' and was the name the Romans gave to a brush used to transfer ink to paper.

5

The history of pencils

Before there were pencils, people drew with burnt sticks. The ancient Egyptians and Romans wrote on papyrus with a thin metal rod called a stylus. It was often made of lead and left a silver mark. People also wrote using ink in quill pens made from feathers. Pencils developed when the dark slippery material called graphite was held in long thin wooden casings and used to make permanent dark, dry marks. These became the pencils we know today.

Pencils through the ages

1662 Friedrich Staedtler is the first to mass-produce pencils in Nuremberg, Germany.

Mid 1500s Solid graphite is discovered at Borrowdale, England. The first pencils are made by wrapping graphite in sheepskin to keep fingers clean, then wrapping it in string to prevent breaking.

1752 In England, graphite is so valuable that stealing it becomes a crime punishable by hard labour or **transportation**. The graphite mines are opened only for six weeks every seven years, to stop the graphite running out.

Early 1800s American Ebenezer Wood automates pencil **manufacturing**.

1500 CE
1600 CE
1700 CE
1800 CE
1815 CE
1830 c

1795 War between France and England cuts off the supply of solid British graphite to France. French chemist Nicolas Conté creates pencil leads by mixing powdered graphite with ground clay and **firing** it, a method still used today.

1761 Kaspar Faber, first of the Faber-Castell pencil-making dynasty, in Germany, makes his first pencils.

Around 1560 In Italy, the first wooden holders are made of juniper wood by Simonio and Lyndiana Bernacotti.

This is the earliest known pencil. It was found in the roof of a house dating back to the 1600s.

A worker at the Faber factory in 1911 cuts wood for pencil casings.

1830
Cumberland graphite becomes so valuable that wooden pencils are filled only halfway with graphite.

1832 Pencils are mass-made at Keswick, England. In 1916, the factory will become the Cumberland Pencil Company and, in 1938, launch Derwent pencils.

Mid 1800s
Jean-Pierre Alibert, a French trader and adventurer, discovers very pure graphite along the Russian–Chinese border.

Mid 1900s
Fourth-generation German pencil manufacturer Lothar Faber uses machines in the family company.

1840 CE · 1850 CE · 1860 CE · 1870 CE · 1880 CE · 1890 CE

1822
Mechanical pencils, which push the lead out gradually, are invented in England.

1835
Johann Sebastian Staedtler opens a pencil factory in Nuremberg, Germany.

1890
Manufacturers begin painting pencils to protect them and make them attractive, and stamp their name on them to advertise their company.

Guess What!

A pencil lead or a line drawn by a pencil will conduct electricity.

What are pencils made from?

'**B**lack-lead' pencils have a thin **cylindrical** core of graphite with an outer casing of wood. The graphite is mixed with clay.

Coloured pencils have a core made from pigments like those in oil and watercolour paints, mixed with waxes and binders to keep it all together.

The casings on pencils are usually painted, **lacquered** and stamped with the name of the manufacturer.

Guess What!

The graphite core in a pencil is sometimes called the 'lead'. It was mistaken for lead because it is shiny. An early name for graphite is *plumbago*, which means 'acts like lead'.

The numbers and letters on pencils show the hardness of the lead.

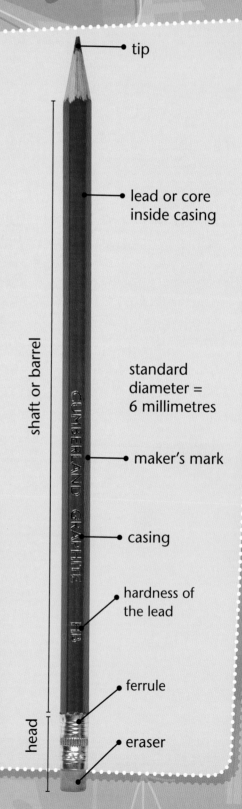

- tip
- lead or core inside casing
- shaft or barrel
- standard diameter = 6 millimetres
- maker's mark
- casing
- hardness of the lead
- ferrule
- eraser
- head

Materials

Many different raw materials are used to make pencils. As with the making of all products, energy is also used to run the machines that help mine the graphite and other minerals, harvest the wood and make the pencils.

Materials needed to make pencils

Material	Purpose and qualities
Wood	Used as the casing of the pencil, which protects the core.
Graphite	Is the major ingredient in the core of the pencil, which makes a mark.
Clay	Mixed with graphite to give the core of the pencil shape and strength.
Wax	Mixed with graphite to make writing smoother.
Glue	Holds the two halves of the casing together.
Paint	Makes the pencil casing attractive, protects it and identifies it.
Lacquer	Protects the paint on the casing.

FABER-CASTELL

Guess What!

On the casing of most pencils, the writing runs from the tip to the head. In pencils made for left-handed people, the writing runs from the head to the tip. To see why, hold a pencil in your left hand.

This Faber-Castell pencil, in Malaysia, is the tallest pencil in the world. It is 19.75 metres high and 0.8 metres around!

Pencil design

Manufacturers make different quality pencils. Cheap pencils may be scratchy to write with and hard to sharpen because they break easily. Pencils made from expensive materials are smoother to use and easier to sharpen. The casings are often beautifully coloured, with as many as ten layers of paint.

Pencils are inexpensive. Cheap pencils may only cost a few cents, but even the most expensive pencils do not cost more than a few dollars.

Pencils are designed for different jobs, such as watercolour pencils for artists, which can be used wet or dry, tiny pencils for card games such as bridge, and flat, soft carpenters' pencils that will not roll away.

Many pencils are round. To prevent them rolling away and help the user grip them well, some companies make pencils that are flat with rounded edges, **hexagonal** or **octagonal**, triangular or even twelve sided.

This high quality pencil has been designed to include a sharpener, an eraser and a pocket clip.

Question & Answer

Why are 75 per cent of American pencils painted yellow?

During the 1890s, the best graphite came from China. American manufacturers used yellow, a colour associated with loyalty and respect in China, to tell customers their pencils contained good-quality Chinese graphite.

Which of these is your favourite pencil?

Novelty pencils

There are many different novelty pencils. They may be very big or very small, have heads shaped like Pinocchio or animals, or be made from twigs. Some pencils are metallic, bendy or even scented.

Novelty pencils may be designed just for fun, or as souvenirs of a place or event. They can also be used to advertise a company, service or product. Some people are fascinated by pencils and collect them.

Question & Answer

What is a mechanical pencil?

Mechanical pencils hold the pencil lead in a metal or plastic holder which pushes the lead out. They produce lines all the same thickness and don't need sharpening.

From wood and graphite to pencils

The process of making everyday objects such as pencils from raw materials involves a large number of steps. In the first stage, the pencil casing and core are prepared. Wood is cut into **slats** and a groove made for the pencil core. The core is made from graphite mixed with clay. This mixture is made into thin rods which are then fired to make them solid and dipped in wax.

In the second stage, the pencil core and its casing are assembled, then cut to size and trimmed. The final stage is finishing the pencils. They may be painted and stamped to give information about the pencil and its manufacturer, and sharpened.

Stage

Stage 1: Preparing the casing and core

Trees are harvested for the pencil casing.

↓

The wood is cut into slats.

↓

Then grooves are cut into the slats.

CASING

Graphite and clay are mined for the pencil core.

↓

Next, the graphite and clay are ground into a powder and mixed together. The graphite is then made into thin rods and fired in a **kiln**.

↓

Lastly, the graphite rods are dipped in a hot wax bath.

CORE

Stage 3: Finishing the pencil

Most pencils are first painted and varnished. Some casings are left natural.

↓

Then the pencils may be stamped to show the maker and the type.

↓

Some pencils have an eraser attached.

↓

Finally, the pencils may be sharpened.

...sembling the casing ...d core

The pencil cores are placed in the grooves in the slats.

↓

Next, the two slats are glued together to form a pencil casing 'sandwich' around the graphite core.

↓

Lastly, the slats are cut into pencils, which are then trimmed to shape.

Question & Answer

Where does the word 'graphite' come from?

The word 'graphite' comes from the Greek word graphein, meaning 'to write'.

Raw materials for pencils

The main raw materials for pencils are graphite, mined from the ground, and wood cut from trees.

Graphite used to be mined in England and America. Today, five countries produce 75 per cent of the world's graphite: China, India, Brazil, Mexico and North Korea.

Pencil casings used to be made mainly from red cedar from Kenya and the United States. Now most pencils are made from incense cedar from Brazil, California, in the United States, and other places. Incense cedar has a long, straight **grain**, which makes pencils easy to manufacture by machine and to sharpen. Some low-priced pencil casing is made from jelutong, a tropical **hardwood** grown in Indonesia and Malaysia.

Question & Answer

How many pencils are made each year in the United States?

2.8 billion, enough to encircle the Earth approximately 15 times if laid end to end.

United Kingdom

France

Germany

Italy

EUROPE

AFRICA

ATLANTIC
OCEAN

INDIA

Trees in a plantation, such as these incense cedars in the United States, are usually all the same species.

Centres for pencil production

Pencils are now made by machine in factories in most countries of the world. In 2005, 52 per cent of the world's pencils were produced in China in just 20 factories. A large number of pencil factories in other countries have been making pencils since the 1800s or earlier. However, some Asian countries, such as Malaysia, India and Japan now have huge modern factories that produce large numbers of pencils very cheaply.

Key

✪ Important graphite-mining countries

◆ Important timber-growing (for pencils) countries

❘ Important pencil-manufacturing countries

ARCTIC OCEAN

✪ Canada

NORTH AMERICA

ATLANTIC OCEAN

✪ North Korea

PACIFIC OCEAN

✪ China

❘ Japan

◆❘ United States of America (California)

❘ Taiwan

✪ Mexico

❘ Thailand

◆ Malaysia

esia ◆ ❘

✪◆ Brazil

SOUTH AMERICA

AUSTRALIA

PACIFIC OCEAN

ATLANTIC OCEAN

HERN OCEAN

This map shows countries that are important to the production of pencils.

ANTARCTICA

Stage 1: Preparing the casing and core

Pencils need a casing and a core or lead.

Casings

First, trees such as incense cedar trees are cut down and machined into large blocks. These blocks are shipped to pencil factories around the world.

The wood is then cut into even slats that will make eight to ten pencils. Each slat is about the length of a pencil and the thickness of half a pencil. This is because two slats will be glued together to make each pencil. The slats are then waxed and stained. Next, evenly spaced grooves are cut into the wood to receive the pencil cores. The grooves are half as deep as the lead is thick.

These slats of wood are about to have grooves cut into them.

Cores

Graphite and clay are found in different places. They are mined from the ground. The graphite and clay are then crushed into powder.

Next, chunks of graphite and clay are mixed in a huge rotating drum to make a dough-like mass. This is squeezed through metal tubes to make thin rods that look like black spaghetti noodles. The noodles are dried carefully in a heating chamber. They are then fired in a kiln at 9400 degrees Celsius to join the ingredients together into a strong core. After this, the cores are dipped in oil or hot wax so that they will write smoothly and not scratch the paper.

A dough of graphite and clay is mixed to make pencil cores.

Guess What!

The cores of coloured pencils are made of clay, waxes, pigments and binders. They are very flexible and rubbery and need to be rolled in cylinders for days to keep their shape while they are being cured or set.

Stage 2: Assembling the casing and core

The pencil cores are placed in the grooves made in the slats. Then two slats are glued together to make a pencil 'sandwich' with cores in the centre of eight to ten pencils. The pencil sandwiches are then glued together under heavy pressure.

This machine assembles the pencil cores and grooved slats.

Guess What!

For the earliest pencil-making, raw graphite was sawn into thin rectangular rods and sandwiched between two pieces of wood. Rectangular cores only needed one side of the casing to be grooved. Round cores need two matching grooves. They have been used from the mid-1870s, when new machines could cut two matching grooves.

Cutting the slats into pencils

When the glue is dry, the slats are cut by machine into pencils. Turning steel blades trim the wood into shape, one side at a time.

This machine cuts the assembled cores and slats into pencils.

Pencil hardnesses

The more graphite, the softer and darker the lead. The more clay, the harder and lighter the lead.

Pencil grading		Colour	Graphite	Clay	Wax
9H	The hardest pencil, with the lightest grey colour		41%	53%	5% *
8H			44%	50%	5%
7H			47%	47%	5%
6H			50%	45%	5%
5H			52%	42%	5%
4H			55%	39%	5%
3H			58%	36%	5%
2H			60%	34%	5%
H	Medium hardness		63%	31%	5%
F	Fine point, medium hardness		66%	28%	5%
HB	Medium hardness		68%	26%	5%
B	Medium hardness		71%	23%	5%
2B			74%	20%	5%
3B			76%	18%	5%
4B			79%	15%	5%
5B			82%	12%	5%
6B			84%	10%	5%
7B			87%	7%	5%
8B	The softest pencil, with the darkest black colour		90%	4%	5%

*Very small amounts of other ingredients make up the final one per cent.

Stage 3: Finishing the pencil

The pencils are sanded to smooth the wood and are usually given coats of paint. They may also be varnished or lacquered, or treated with an ultra-violet process to keep the paint bright.

Words can be stamped on the pencils using a metal stamp with pigments and resin. These may show the maker, the name of the sort of pencil and its hardness.

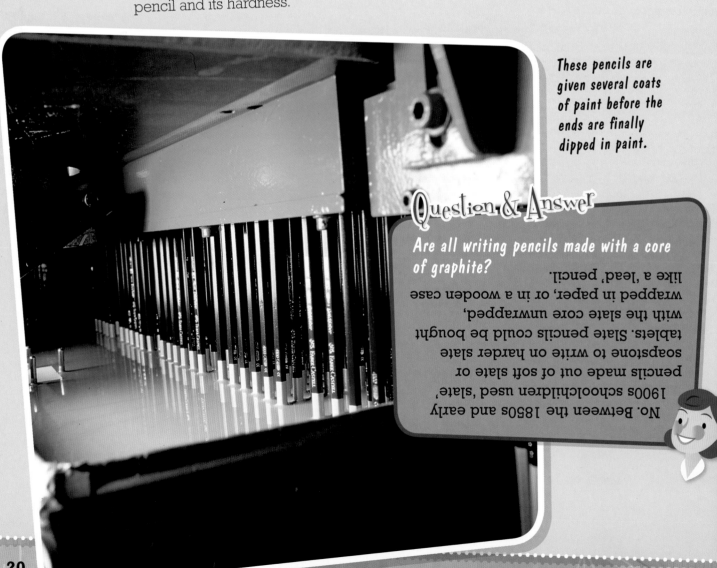

These pencils are given several coats of paint before the ends are finally dipped in paint.

Question & Answer

Are all writing pencils made with a core of graphite?

No. Between the 1850s and early 1900s schoolchildren used 'slate' pencils made out of soft slate or soapstone to write on harder slate tablets. Slate pencils could be bought with the slate core unwrapped, wrapped in paper, or in a wooden case like a 'lead' pencil.

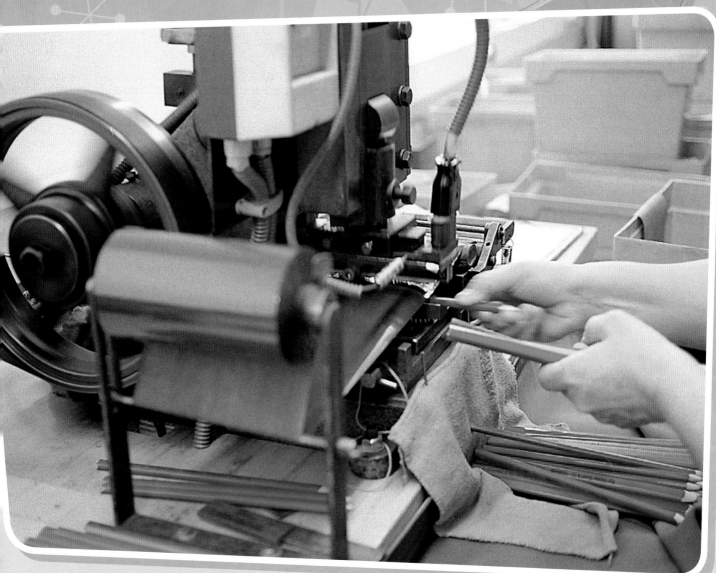

The final decoration for these carpenter's pencils is stamped on by hand.

Finishing touches

If an eraser is being attached to the pencil, a groove is cut around the wood at the head of the pencil. A metal clamp called a ferrule is used to attach the rubber to the end of the pencil. Ferrules are usually made of brass (a mixture of zinc and copper).

In many countries, the pencil is sharpened in the factory before being sold. This may be done with strips of emery board, a material like sandpaper. English pencils are generally sold unsharpened.

Question & Answer

How long a line can an average pencil draw? How many words can it write?

An average pencil can draw a line 56 kilometres long, or write 45 000 words.

Packaging and distribution

Products are packaged to protect them while they are being transported. Packaging also displays the maker's brand and makes products look attractive when they are sold.

Pencils may be sold loose, or in cardboard, plastic or wooden boxes, depending on their quality.

Coloured pencils are often packaged in unusual ways, such as in round tins, to attract children. Tins and other packages are often shrink-wrapped in plastic.

Whichever way they are packaged, the pencils must be protected from damage, especially if they are sharpened. The packaged pencils are then packed in bigger boxes. Some packaging is made from recycled paper.

These high quality artist's pencils are protected in a tin.

Distribution

From factories, pencils are shipped around the world. Their journey may involve ships, planes and trucks. Pencils are often sold to **wholesalers**, who buy large quantities to sell to **distributors**.

The pencils are then stored in the distibutors' warehouses, waiting to be sold to supermarkets, stationery stores, art shops, chain stores, souvenir stores and small shops.

Pencil manufacturers often supply special packaging or racks for shops to display their pencils.

Question & Answer

How many pencils does a tree produce?

A 14-year-old Pinus caribaea tree is able to produce 2500 pencils.

Cross-Hatching   Texture   Bracelet Shading   Tonal Drawing   Sfumato

REXEL

23

Marketing and advertising

Marketing and advertising are used to promote and sell products.

Marketing

Many different people buy pencils and there are different markets for different pencils. Expensive pencils are sold to artists and those who want quality products. Workers such as carpenters need special pencils. Large pencils and pencils with special grips are made for young children.

This colourful display of pencils at a toy store in Japan is designed to appeal to children.

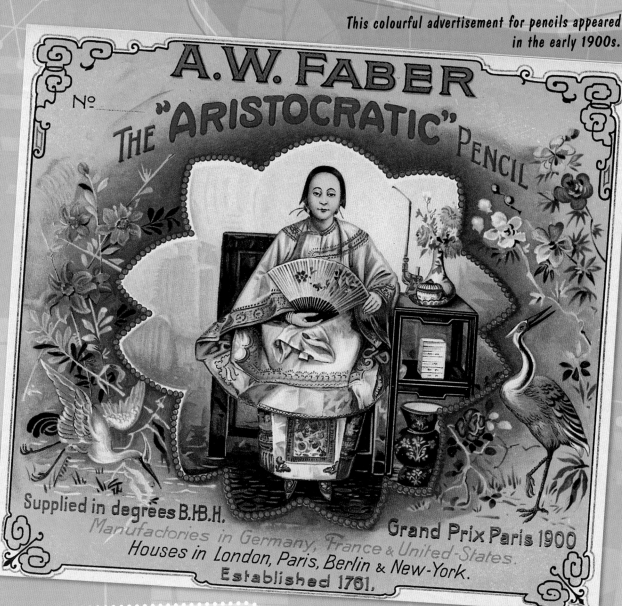

Advertising

In the first half of the 1900s, pencils used to be advertised by themselves in newspapers and other print media. Now, pencils are generally advertised with other products as part of 'back-to-school specials' brochures.

Some more expensive pencils and collectors' items are sold over the Internet.

Guess What!

Different countries have different traditional colours for the barrels of graphite pencils.

Country	Pencil casing colour
Argentina	Black (low cost pencils)
Australia	Usually red
Brazil	Green and black
England	Varies
Germany	Green (based on the trademark colour of Faber-Castell)
	Yellow (low-cost Staedtler pencils)
	Red and black (higher quality Staedtler pencils)
United States	Yellow

Production of pencils

Products may be made in factories in huge quantities. This is called mass production. They can also be made in small quantities by hand, by skilled craftspeople.

Mass production

When pencils were first manufactured, they were made by hand by people working at home, doing all parts of the process. This is called a cottage industry.

Now, pencils are mass produced by machines. Machines make processes quicker, easier and cheaper. Each pencil is exactly the same, and the quality can be controlled more easily.

Mass-produced pencils are all of exactly the same high quality.

Guess What!

Lead pencils were used on board the United States' 'Mercury' and 'Gemini' space missions, and are still used aboard the *International Space Station*. In a spacecraft, however, pencil tips can break off and float into eyes, noses or equipment. So Fisher, a manufacturer, developed a pen that worked by pressure and would write in zero gravity. Developing the pen cost a million dollars, but Fisher sold them very cheaply to NASA. His reward was publicity.

Small-scale production

Handmade pencils are generally made either from twigs that have been bored to accept a pencil core, or from wood shaped on a machine called a lathe. Sometimes, wood from special structures that have been demolished, such as sports stadiums, are made into souvenir pencils. There are also handmade pencils whose shaft is made from plastic.

Handmade pencils are valued because each one is unique. Attention is paid to the way each pencil looks.

Some artists have used pencils to make art. They have made pencils into sculptures, jewellery and even clothing and hats!

A handmade pencil like this is valued for its uniqueness.

Pencils and the environment

Making any product affects the environment. It also affects the people who make the product. It is important to think about the impact of a product through its entire life cycle. This includes getting the raw materials, making the product and disposing of it. Any problems need to be worked on so products can be made in the best ways available.

Mines and metal production

Ideally, products are made from **renewable resources**, that is, materials that will not run out.

Graphite is a non-renewable resource, because once all the graphite has been mined, there will not be any more. Artificial graphite, however, has been made from other renewable materials.

The wood for pencil casings comes from **plantations** of incense cedar, which are farmed sustainably. This means that when trees are cut down, other trees are planted in a way that protects wildlife, plants, soil, water and air quality.

Growing plantations of incense cedars rather than cutting trees from wild forests is a sustainable way of supplying wood for pencil casings.

Always sharpen your pencils with a sharp pencil sharpener, otherwise the wood can be damaged.

Recycling

It is hard to recycle pencils, but pencil shavings can be made into **compost.**

Choosing to use pencils rather than pens or computers also means using less non-renewable materials such as plastic and ink, and metals that need to be mined.

Questions to think about

We need to conserve the raw materials used to produce even ordinary objects such as pencils. Making items from renewable resources, conserving energy and preventing pollution as much as possible means there will be enough resources in the future and a cleaner environment.

These are some questions you might like to think about:

❄ How can manufacturers reduce the amount of non-renewable raw materials that make pencils?

❄ Which company makes the largest range of coloured pencils you can buy?

❄ What pencils can you buy that will use the least non-renewable raw materials?

❄ What is your favourite pencil? Why?

❄ How can you make sure you use your pencils as fully as possible?

❄ What is the best way of recycling pencil shavings?

Do you have a favourite pencil to write and draw with?

Glossary

compost
decayed material used to fertilise plants

cylindrical
shaped with long sides and circular ends

distributors
shops or wholesalers that have the right to sell a particular product in a certain area

ferrule
metal ring that holds an eraser onto a pencil

firing
heating in a kiln

grain
the direction wood fibres lie in

graphite
form of carbon used to make pencil leads

hardwood
tree containing short fibres (1 millimetre long) such as eucalypt, acacia and birch

hexagonal
six-sided

kiln
a very hot oven

lacquered
covered in a transparent, hard coating

manufacturing
making, mainly by machine

octagonal
eight-sided

pigments
substances used for colouring

plantations
forests planted by people for harvesting

renewable resources
resources that can easily be grown or made again

slats
thin pieces of wood

transportation
punishment by being sent overseas to a prison colony

wholesalers
businesses that buy very large quantities of goods and sell them to shops, rather than directly to the consumer

Index